You'd Better...

by Patrick Cooper

Illustrated by Nick Ward

Chapter 1

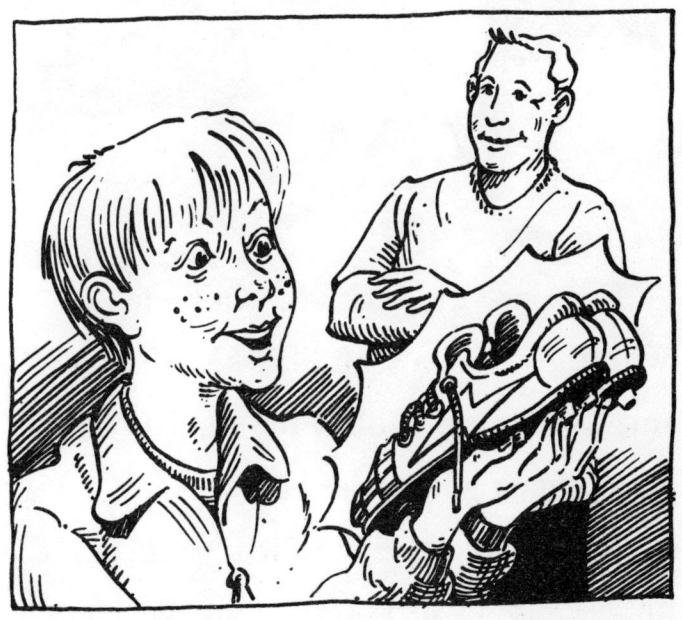

Uncle Pete gave me my boots. We went and bought them together. They were "Blades". Everything else I had was always cheap, but Uncle Pete understood about football. He knew what it meant to have good boots.

I ran into the park and put them on. With those boots I felt like the ball was stuck with elastic to my toe-caps. I could do anything with those boots.

Maybe Uncle Pete wanted to cheer me up, because I wasn't too happy. We had just moved. Where we lived before, I knew all the kids in the street. We played non-stop football. Now I hardly knew anyone, except Gina from next door. Also, I started at a new school and didn't like it. The kids teased me because I'm small.

Mr Edwards ran the school football team. I asked him if I could be in it. He looked down his nose at me.

"I practise loads. I've got skill," I said.

Look, laddie, in our team, you'd be squashed flat. Go home and grow!

So I went and played in the park with Gina.

Gina is the opposite of me. She's really tall. She's still getting taller. Her mum says she should play basketball, not football. But Gina loves football. She's not as quick as me with her feet, but she's brilliant with her head. She can nod the ball any way she wants. She's cool.

But I wanted to be in a team. I wanted to play in matches.

Uncle Pete knew that. So he found out about the Swallows, and sent me to see Mr Palmer.

The Swallows aren't anything to do with school. They play in the Junior League on Saturdays. Mr Palmer was their new manager.

Mr Palmer had taken on the worst team in the history of football. The Swallows always lost.

THE SWALLOWS
Record for this season:

PLAYED	WON	DRAWN	LOST	GOALS FOR	GOALS AGAINST
10	0	0	10	6	127

I went to see Mr Palmer after school.

"Oh, I'm sorry," he said. "I thought you were older. You've got to be thirteen to play in our team."

"I'm fourteen," I said. I felt rotten. I must have looked pathetic too. Mr Palmer took pity on me.

"What's your name?" he asked.

"Jason," I said.

"All right, Jason. Come to training on Thursday and we'll take a look."

I ran home punching the air. I knew that once he saw me play he'd have to pick me.

The only thing was ...

Chapter 2

... he didn't!

Training was in a gym. When I walked in, everybody looked at me as if I'd come to the wrong place by mistake.

Mr Palmer said, "This is Jason. Jason's joining the team. We're going to start winning now."

Some of the boys laughed.

"I mean it," he said.

"He can't be in the team," said Liam. "Look at him. He's not thirteen. He's probably still at play group."

They laughed again. But Harry, who's in my class, said, "He is old enough. He's just small."

"If he's good enough, he's big enough," said Mr Palmer. "The best player in the world at the moment is Juninho, and he is 5 feet, 5 inches. Got it? Now let's go. Next Saturday's team play like elephants: all push, no skill. We have a real chance. All we have to do is play as a team. That means knowing your positions, supporting each other. Pass and move. And believe in yourselves!"

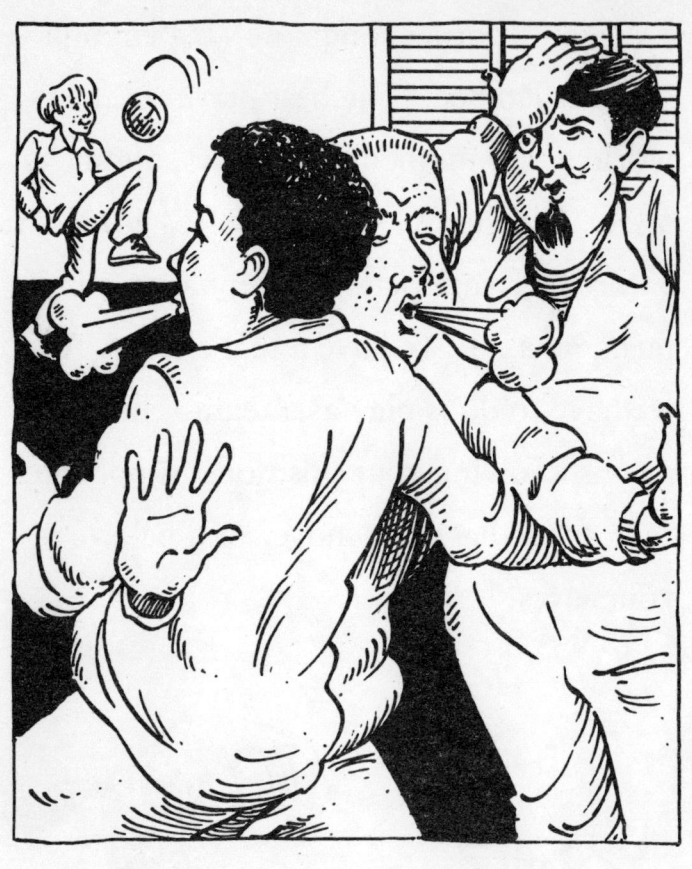

I enjoyed the training a lot. One thing about Mr Palmer was that he never yelled at anyone. That was hard, the way the Swallows played. I was the best on the ball, so I was sure I would be in the team.

But at the end of training Mr Palmer took me aside.

"Well done, Jason," he said. "Look, don't take it the wrong way, but I want you to be substitute on Saturday."

My face fell.

"Aren't I good enough?" I asked.

"Oh yes, you're good enough all right. But it's a tough game at this level, and it's not just skill that counts. I want to let you in slowly."

He was saying I was too small. Just like Mr Edwards.

Chapter 3

On Saturday, I saw why the Swallows always lost. It was because they were useless. They didn't even try to control the ball, or pass it to each other. Whatever Mr Palmer said, once they got on the field they just rushed after the ball and kicked it all over the place. Or else they daydreamed.

It was sad.

The silly thing was, they weren't really bad players.

Alf played on the wing.
He could kick hard.

Liam was a back.
He got in the way well.

Mikey and Harry
tried hard.

Jamie was really good. He saved loads of goals and kept us smiling. You needed a sense of humour to be the Swallows' goalkeeper.

What do you call Eric Cantona with bananas in his ears?

Anything you like. He can't hear you!

But the best player was Ed, the striker. He had a great shot.

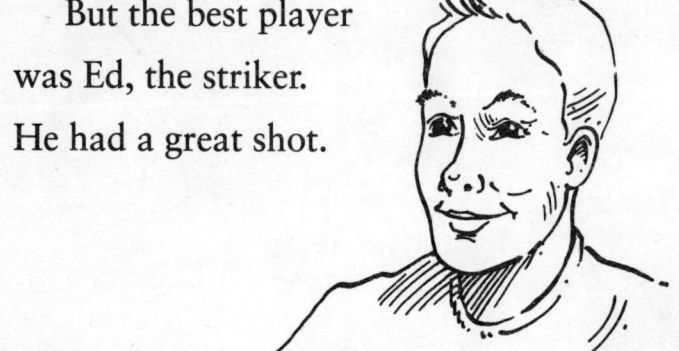

Mr Palmer ran up and down the line, puffing and panting and shouting.

"Well tried, Alf! Good lads! Keep it up! Nice one, Mikey!"

The other manager ran up and down too. He didn't seem very happy.

"Pull your finger out! That was pathetic!"

By half-time the other side were only 3–0 up. Swallows were doing well! But then we fell apart, and suddenly it was 7–0.

Ed had hardly been near the ball.

Then it happened. Mr Palmer came up to me.

"I'm sending you on, Jason," he said. "Hold the middle of the park and get the ball to Ed."

A moment later, I was on. I was wearing my new boots, my "Blades".

Playing in the team! For ten minutes.

Cool!

The big guys on the other team all laughed when I came on.

"Look at this little twerp! Stick a dummy in his mouth!"

"Nah, he'll dribble!"

I didn't care. What did they know?

Anyway, after a minute they forgot about me, and nobody bothered to mark me. Then the ball bounced towards me. Ed was running back, but I collected it first. I ran up the pitch. There was nobody for miles. Their defenders had all gone to sleep. Ed was on my left. A couple of

defenders came to life and charged at me. I flicked the ball towards Ed's head. He rose up, one head above everybody else's. He connected perfectly. The ball flew past the keeper's hands, into the top of the net.

GOAL!!!

It was easy!

Mr Palmer looked like he was going to explode. The other coach was screaming.

I didn't take any notice. I was used to that. But the next time I got the ball I did get squashed. I knew then why Mr Palmer

had been worried. This big guy just ran at me. He didn't play the ball. He just knocked me over and sat on me. We got a free kick, but by the time I had my breath back, the game was over.

I felt better, though, when the whole team came up to me, grinning and patting me on the back.

"We'll show 'em next Saturday, eh Jase?" said Ed.

I wanted to believe him.

Chapter 4

Next Saturday we were playing the only team in the league who were as bad as we were. If we beat them we might not finish bottom. Me and Ed passed the ball about, and we ran rings round them. And we won! 3–1! Ed scored two goals, and Alf scored one, his first ever. He was over the moon!

The week after that, we went to the match in a minibus. Jamie turned up in a green wig and told us bad jokes all the way.

This time, the other team were older than us, they were bigger than us, and they were good. They thought they were going to walk all over us.

But they didn't.

Everyone got stuck in, and Jamie made some amazing saves. At half-time they had only scored one goal. Their manager was yelling at them. Mr Palmer couldn't believe it.

You boys, you're ... you're ...

He was lost for words. Then we went back on, and Ed scored a goal. We went crazy! The way Ed was playing, we thought we could beat anybody now!

It was too good to last. They just went for Ed after that. They marked him out of the game. He tried to make space. Then disaster struck: Ed fell hard. He lay on the

ground holding his leg. Mr Palmer took Ed's arm over his shoulder and helped him to hobble off.

That was it. From then on we played like rabbits. We lost that game 7–1. But it was worse than that. Ed had pulled a hamstring. He wouldn't be able to play again for at least a month.

Ed went off to the doctor with his Dad. We went home in the minibus. We had lost our striker and our best player.

"Don't worry," said Mr Palmer. "We'll find someone else just as good."

"There isn't anyone," said Liam.

I knew someone. She was brilliant. But I knew what they would say.

Chapter 5

"Gina can't play with us. She's a girl!"

It was little Mikey. He was almost as small as me. He had a kid sister who always wore pink, and made Mikey get the blame for things.

Some of the boys agreed with him. Gina looked disgusted. She was going to walk straight out. Mr Palmer called us together.

"Look," he said. "Let's not have any nonsense. We want to win. Three weeks ago you didn't want Jason, because he was small. You can't say Gina's too small, can you? If she's good enough, she plays. Now let's get on with training."

Some of the boys nodded. The rest looked at their feet. Gina was grinning again.

I looked across at Mikey and Liam and the other boys trying to be tough, and I realized they were scared of Gina.

They didn't need to be. She was on their side.

Next Saturday, we were playing at home. Uncle Pete took me and Gina to the playing field.

"Go for it!" he said. "You guys could beat 'em single handed."

"We don't play with our hands, Uncle Pete," I said.

When the other team saw Gina, their jaws dropped. Then they started laughing and pointing. They had a mean-looking defender. I called him Vinny. He put his hands on his hips and shouted.

They laughed, but they were worried. Gina was bigger than any of them.

"Keep going forward," said Mr Palmer. "Don't panic. Believe in yourselves! You can win."

The game started. They moved into our penalty area, and we panicked. Gina hung about on the half-way line looking lost, waiting for a touch.

Jamie made a brilliant save. That cheered us up for a moment. Then he made another, and another.

It couldn't go on.

It didn't. Someone shot, the ball bounced off Liam, and Jamie never had a chance.

1–0.

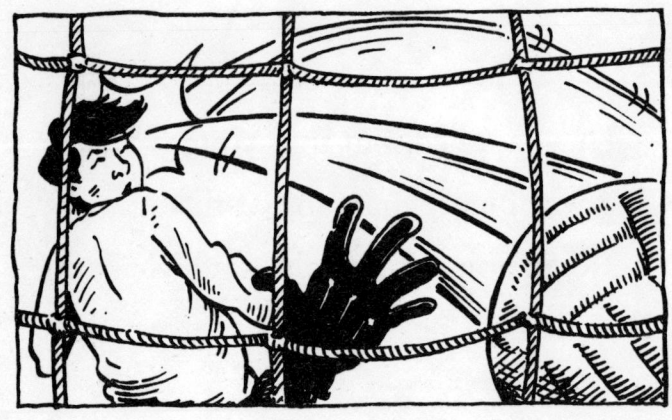

At kick-off I tried a move we'd practised. I passed the ball to Alf on the wing. He was supposed to cross it for Gina to run on to. Simple! Only Alf was asleep, and their winger picked up my pass. He ran straight through and scored again.

2–0.

It was depressing. Gina was kicking her feet and looking bored. Vinny was meant to be marking me, but he kept going up to Gina and pestering her. It was sad, but it was getting to her. We were playing worse and worse.

"Get back!" Mr Palmer shouted to Gina. "Stay with Jason! Support each other!"

Then Vinny did something really stupid. We gave away a corner. Just as the kick was taken, Vinny came up behind Gina. He said, "Do you like playing with the boys then, babe?" and kicked her on the shin.

Her eyes rolled and her jaw set. And at that moment the ball came to her and she was off.

Nobody could have stopped Gina. Nobody could come within a mile of her!

She ran through eight of their players, and round the goalkeeper. She only stopped when she and the ball were both inside the back of the net.

Then she turned and gave me the biggest grin of her life.

2–1! And all the boys were mobbing her.

Mr Palmer exploded again. All our boys were leaping around like frogs. They forgot about the game. Stupid, because the other team came straight back, and scored another goal.

3–1.

"Play as a team!" shouted Mr Palmer. "Believe you can do it!"

And we did! It started with me and Gina and Alf. Alf centred the ball. Gina nodded the ball to me. I passed it back to Alf. We just kept the ball. Soon the other boys got the idea. And instead of rushing after the ball and never getting it, we supported each other. We passed and moved.

We couldn't get a goal, though. The other team were marking Gina like a Maths test. There was no way she was going to get through.

Then Gina saw little Mikey. He had run through on the left. So instead of passing back to me, which everyone was expecting, she nodded it forward, and it landed at Mikey's feet. Mikey ran a few yards, and booted it as hard as he could.

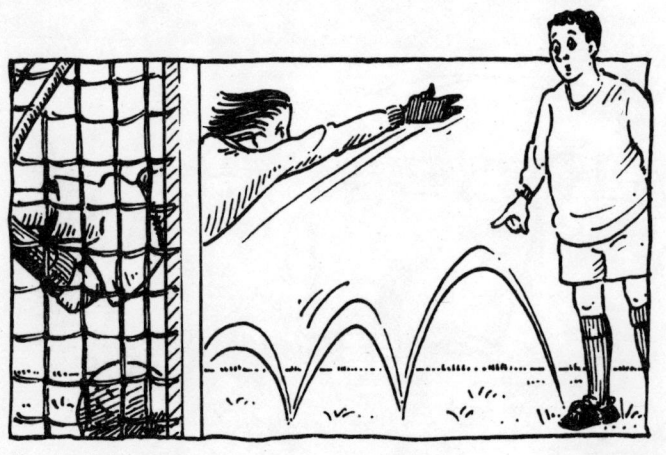

That wasn't very hard, but it dribbled in the right direction. The keeper flung himself across the goal, dived at the ball, and knocked it over the line. The whistle blew!

3–2!

Mikey looked like he'd won the cup final.

After that they put the pressure back on us. Vinny had me marked tight. Gina was squeezed out. They were still a goal ahead and time was running out. They thought they'd won.

Then Liam started to help me. He had never done anything like that before, he was just good at getting in the way. I think he hated Vinny. He blocked him and stopped him getting near me. Vinny was furious, but Liam wasn't that easy to get round. It meant I finally got the ball, and a bit of space.

There were four big kids in front of me, but they were slow. I dummied to Alf. Then I ran at them.

I twisted. I ducked. I dodged. The ball stuck to my "Blades".

I turned them all, until there was only me and one defender, and the goalkeeper running out at me. Oh, and Gina on my right.

I flicked the ball up, good and high.

Gina's head was just where it ought to be. She made perfect contact.

The ball curled and dipped. The keeper dived, but he was nowhere near it as it skimmed under the bar, into the back of the net.

3–3! Gina scored, but I made it!

The whistle blew. The match was a draw.

It wasn't like a draw for us, though. It was an amazing victory!

Chapter 6

After that game we never looked back. We weren't even second bottom at the end of the season, we were third from bottom! Ed came back for the last few games, and with him and Gina together up front, no one thought the Swallows were a walk-over.

This season, Ed is too old for the Swallows. But Gina has played every game, and nobody laughs – not when they see how she plays. She's the top goal scorer in the league so far, and Swallows are fifth.

As for me, I'm captain of the Swallows now, and I also play in the school team with Ed. No one makes jokes about my size, though I wouldn't care if they did. I've grown out of my "Blades", so I've hung them on my wall. They helped make thirty-six goals, and scored seven.

The Swallows are going to win the league this year.

You'd better believe it!